D0540651

Wise Words to Obey

Words of wisdom from the
Book of Proverbs

Carine Mackenzie
Illustrated by Helen Smith

Commit your works
to the Lord, and
your thoughts will
be established.
Proverbs 16:3

For whoever finds me
finds life,
and obtains favour
from the LORD.
Proverbs 8:35

Keep your heart with all diligence, for out of it spring the issues of life.
Proverbs 4:23

If we store up good things in our heart, and think about what is true and right and pure, then our words and actions will be good too. Pray that the Lord Jesus will keep your heart fixed on him.

PRAYER

Dear Lord Jesus, I find it easy to think bad thoughts. Please help me to think about things that are good and true and especially about you and all you have done for me. Amen.

**The kind man does good for
his own soul. But he who is cruel
troubles his own flesh.
Proverbs 11:17**

Do you like helping mum or grandpa in the kitchen or garden? God wants us to be kind and helpful in all we do.

Prayer
Please help me, Lord God, to be kind and helpful. I am sorry when I am selfish and won't share. Amen.

As cold water to a weary soul, so is good news from a far country.
Proverbs 25:25

Hearing good news from a friend who is far away, makes us happy. It is as refreshing as a lovely drink of cold water when we are very thirsty. The best news of all is from God who tells us about the Lord Jesus, the Saviour.

PRAYER

Lord, thank you for the different ways that we can hear news from far away - the post, the telephone, e-mails. Thank you for the best news of all, the gospel, telling us about the Lord Jesus Christ who died to save us from our sins. I need him. Amen.

The eyes of the LORD are in every place, keeping watch on the evil and the good.
Proverbs 15:3

God knows everything and everybody all over the world. He sees each person in every country in the world. God loved the world so much, he sent his only Son here so that those who trust in him would have eternal life.

PRAYER

Lord, you see everyone and know
what we are doing. No one can hide
from you. Help me to remember that
and to trust in you. Amen.

The righteous should choose his friends carefully, for the way of the wicked leads them astray.
Proverbs 12:26

Say thank you to God for your friends. It is good to spend time with people who will not tempt you to sin and turn away from God. Pray that you will be a good and wise friend.

PRAYER
Thank you, Lord, for my friends.
Help me to be a good friend. Thank
you most of all for the best friend,
the Lord Jesus. Amen.

A friend loves at all times.
Proverbs 17:17

A really good friend will still be your friend even when you are sad or don't feel like playing or have no special toys. The best friend of all is the Lord Jesus who never leaves us.

PRAYER

Dear Lord, sometimes I feel lonely or grumpy or sad. Help me to think of you and know that you are always with me, my best friend. Amen.

The words of a gossip are like tasty morsels, and they go down into the inmost body.
Proverbs 18:8

If someone says something nasty about you, you know how deeply hurt you feel. Remember how much God has forgiven you through the life and death of the Lord Jesus.

PRAYER

Lord, help me to think before I speak
an unkind word or pass on a story
about someone. Help me to forgive
as I remember how much you have
forgiven me. Amen.

A man who isolates himself seeks his own desire, he rages against all wise judgement.
Proverbs 18:1

How happy the children look when they are playing together. The boy who is on the side keeping apart does not look happy. It is sometimes hard to join in with others. Try to be nice to new children so that they don't feel awkward or unhappy.

PRAYER

Oh Lord, I am sorry that I fight with my friends and sulk sometimes. Help me please to say sorry to them and to you. Amen.

To do righteousness and justice is
more acceptable to the
LORD than sacrifice.
Proverbs 21:3

The little girl has broken the window. She could
have run away but instead she owns up to the
man in the house. This was the right and fair
thing to do. The Lord God is pleased by this
behaviour.

PRAYER

Lord, please help me to say sorry when I do something wrong. Thank you that you promise to forgive if we confess our sin and turn to you. Amen.

Every word of God is
pure; he is a shield to
those who put their
trust in him.
Proverbs 30:5

For the LORD gives
wisdom; from His
mouth come knowledge
and understanding.
Proverbs 2:6

© Copyright 2009 Carine Mackenzie
ISBN: 978-1-84550-431-1
Scripture quotations are based
on the New King James Version.
Published by Christian Focus Publications,
Geanies House, Fearn, Tain, Ross-shire, IV20 1TW,
Scotland, U.K.
www.christianfocus.com
Illustrated by Helen Smith
Cover design by Daniel van Straaten
Printed in China

Themes in this book:

Commitment: Page 2, 3, 4
Obedience: Page 6, 10, 22
Forgiveness: Page 16, 20
Friendship: Page 12, 14, 18
Good news: Page 8
Wisdom: Page 23

Themes of other books in the series:

Wise Words to Trust, ISBN 978-1-84550-432-8
Comfort, discipline, kindness, obedience,
safety, wisdom.

Wise Words to Follow, ISBN 978-1-84550-430-4
Caring, God's blessing, guidance, listening and
learning, obedience, rest and refreshment.